IT'S TIME TO LEARN ABOUT BUTTERFLIES AND MOTHS

It's Time to Learn about Butterflies and Moths

Walter the Educator

Silent King Books
A WhichHead Entertainment Imprint

Copyright © 2025 by Walter the Educator

All rights reserved. No part of this book may be reproduced in any manner whatsoever without written per- mission except in the case of brief quotations embodied in critical articles and reviews.

First Printing, 2024

Disclaimer

This book is a literary work; the story is not about specific persons, locations, situations, and/or circumstances unless mentioned in a historical context. Any resemblance to real persons, locations, situations, and/or circumstances is coincidental. This book is for entertainment and informational purposes only. The author and publisher offer this information without warranties expressed or implied. No matter the grounds, neither the author nor the publisher will be accountable for any losses, injuries, or other damages caused by the reader's use of this book. The use of this book acknowledges an understanding and acceptance of this disclaimer.

It's Time to Learn about Butterflies and Moths is a collectible early learning book by Walter the Educator suitable for all ages belonging to Walter the Educator's Time to Eat Book Series. Collect more books at WaltertheEducator.com

USE THE EXTRA SPACE TO TAKE NOTES AND DOCUMENT YOUR MEMORIES

BUTTERFLIES AND MOTHS

Butterflies dance in the bright sunlight,

It's Time to Learn about

Butterflies and Moths

With wings so bold, a shining sight.

Moths flutter softly in the night,

Their colors calm, not big and bright.

Butterflies love the flowers at noon,

Sipping sweet nectar with their spoon.

Moths like the moon and the dark sky,

Flying where owls and fireflies fly.

Butterflies rest with wings held high,

Like folded hands up toward the sky.

Moths lay their wings down flat and wide,

A quiet place for them to hide.

Butterflies come in colors galore,

Blues and reds and so much more!

Moths wear browns and greys so light,

Perfect for blending into the night.

It's Time to Learn about
Butterflies and Moths

Butterflies' antennae are thin and neat,

With little clubs at the end so sweet.

Moths have antennae feathery and wide,

Like soft little combs on either side.

Both start as eggs so tiny and round,

On leaves or branches close to the ground.

Then comes the caterpillar's munch,

Eating leaves for lunch and brunch!

Wrapped in cocoons or chrysalis tight,

They change their forms, hidden from sight.

Butterflies wear a chrysalis thin,

While moths spin cocoons to tuck in.

Out they come with wings so new,

Drying off in the sun or dew.

Butterflies fly where the flowers glow,

It's Time to Learn about
Butterflies and Moths

Moths flap softly when night winds blow.

Though they look alike in many ways,

Their habits and lives make them stray.

Butterflies love the sunny air,

While moths find nighttime cool and fair.

Now you know these fluttering friends,

With wings that shine or gently blend.

Butterflies and moths both share,

It's Time to Learn about
Butterflies and Moths

The gift of flight, light as air!

ABOUT THE CREATOR

Walter the Educator is one of the pseudonyms for Walter Anderson. Formally educated in Chemistry, Business, and Education, he is an educator, an author, a diverse entrepreneur, and he is the son of a disabled war veteran. "Walter the Educator" shares his time between educating and creating. He holds interests and owns several creative projects that entertain, enlighten, enhance, and educate, hoping to inspire and motivate you. Follow, find new works, and stay up to date with Walter the Educator™

at WaltertheEducator.com

www.ingramcontent.com/pod-product-compliance
Lightning Source LLC
LaVergne TN
LVHW051919060526
838201LV00060B/4079